THE FBI STORY

The FBI and Civil Rights

By Dale Anderson

MASON CREST PUBLISHERS

Produced in association with Water Buffalo Books.
Design by Westgraphix LLC.

MASON CREST PUBLISHERS INC.
370 Reed Road
Broomall, Pennsylvania 19008
(866) MCP-BOOK (toll free)
www.masoncrest.com

Printed in the United States of America

First Printing

9 8 7 6 5 4 3 2 1

Library of Congress Cataloging-in-Publication Data

Anderson, Dale, 1953-
      The FBI and civil rights / Dale Anderson.
         p. cm. — (The FBI story)
      Includes bibliographical references and index.
      ISBN 978-1-4222-0569-3 (hardcover : alk. paper) — ISBN 978-1-4222-1368-1 (pbk.: alk. paper)
  1. United States. Federal Bureau of Investigation—Juvenile literature. 2. Civil rights—United States—
Juvenile literature. 3. Criminal investigation—United States—Juvenile literature. I. Title.
  HV8144.F43A53 2008
  363.25'95—dc22   2008047899

Publisher's note:
All quotations in this book come from original sources and contain the spelling and grammatical
inconsistencies of the original text.

CONTENTS

Mississippi Burning

In the summer of 1964, hundreds of **civil rights** workers gathered in Mississippi. Their goal was to help African Americans in that state register to vote. Their drive was meant to end decades of unequal treatment suffered by blacks. For many years, whites had controlled state and local governments in Mississippi and across the South. They had used their positions in power to pass laws that denied black Americans basic rights. The civil rights workers saw voter **registration** as a vital step in ending this injustice. They believed that if blacks had the power to vote, **discrimination** against them would end. Politicians would have to pay attention to their concerns in order to get

As part of the 1964 "Freedom Summer" (also known as the Mississippi Summer Project), civil rights workers helped register black voters who had been denied the vote by discriminatory laws. Others started tutoring programs. At right, a volunteer speaks with children.

elected. The civil rights workers called their campaign "Freedom Summer."

The summer would be dangerous for those workers, however. Some white **extremists** did not believe that the different races were equal. They wanted to maintain the system of **segregation** in Mississippi. Some of these extremists belonged to a secret group called the **Ku Klux Klan**. These men attacked civil rights workers. They wore white robes and masks to hide who they

Ku Klux Klan members rally in a field in Mississippi. The KKK used threats and violence, including murder, to intimidate African-American voters in the South and civil rights workers trying to help them.

were. They often struck at night, trying to instill fear and drive the civil rights **activists** away.

Disappearance and Suspicion

On June 21, 1964, three civil rights workers were arrested for speeding near the town of Philadelphia, Mississippi. Two of them—Michael Schwerner and Andrew Goodman—were whites from New York. The third, James Chaney, was a black man from Meridian, Mississippi. The three were held in county jail for a few hours and then released. Soon after their release—around 10:30 that night—they disappeared.

Given the dangerous conditions for civil rights workers in the South, other civil rights workers feared that the three men were dead. Certain they would get no help from state police, they called the Federal Bureau of Investigation. On June 22, FBI agents arrived in the area from the New Orleans **field office**. Harry Maynor, heading the team, vowed, "We're going to see if we can find those guys."

Still, the FBI moved slowly at first. For decades, FBI Director J. Edgar Hoover had considered **communists** and members of other political and social groups as grave threats to the nation as a whole. He suspected civil rights leader Martin Luther King, Jr., of having ties with communists, and by the early 1960s, when the civil rights movement began to build in strength, Hoover had his agents busy spying on King and other leaders of the civil rights movement. Pressure began to build on President Lyndon Johnson to do more to find the missing workers in Mississippi. When Johnson pushed Hoover to open an FBI field office in Jackson, Mississippi, and to send more agents to work on the case, Hoover did so, reluctantly.

Bodies Found

Although Hoover was not strongly committed to handling this case, his agents were determined to find out what happened. They dug deeply.

FBI inspector Joseph Sullivan led the investigation. It was code-named MIBURN, short for "Mississippi Burning." The name referred to the firebombing of an African-American church that had taken place earlier in the year. Along with looking for the three civil rights workers, the FBI investigated that church fire. They also investigated the beatings of other civil rights workers and other similar cases in the

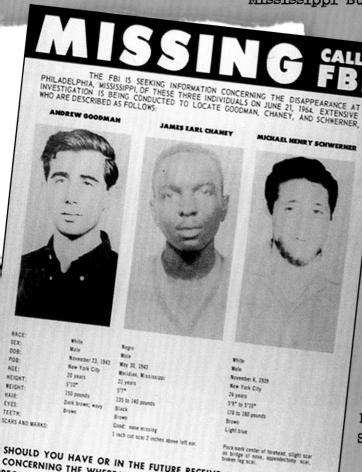

MISSING CALL FBI

THE FBI IS SEEKING INFORMATION CONCERNING THE DISAPPEARANCE AT PHILADELPHIA, MISSISSIPPI, OF THESE THREE INDIVIDUALS ON JUNE 21, 1964. EXTENSIVE INVESTIGATION IS BEING CONDUCTED TO LOCATE GOODMAN, CHANEY, AND SCHWERNER, WHO ARE DESCRIBED AS FOLLOWS:

ANDREW GOODMAN   JAMES EARL CHANEY   MICHAEL HENRY SCHWERNER

RACE:	White	Negro	
SEX:	Male	Male	White
DOB:	November 23, 1943	May 30, 1943	Male
POB:	New York City	Meridian, Mississippi	November 6, 1929
AGE:	20 years	21 years	New York City
HEIGHT:	5'10"	5'7"	24 years
WEIGHT:	150 pounds	135 to 140 pounds	5'9" to 5'10"
HAIR:	Dark brown; wavy	Black	170 to 180 pounds
EYES:	Brown	Brown	Brown
TEETH:		Good; none missing	Light blue
SCARS AND MARKS:		1 inch cut scar 2 inches above left ear.	Pock mark center of forehead, slight scar on bridge of nose, appendectomy scar, broken leg scar.

SHOULD YOU HAVE OR IN THE FUTURE RECEIVE ANY INFORMATION CONCERNING THE WHEREABOUTS OF THESE INDIVIDUALS, YOU ARE REQUESTED TO NOTIFY ME OR THE NEAREST OFFICE OF THE FBI. TELEPHONE NUMBER IS LISTED BELOW.

29, 1964

DIRECTOR
FEDERAL BUREAU OF INVESTIGATION
UNITED STATES DEPARTMENT OF JUSTICE
WASHINGTON, D. C. 20535
TELEPHONE, NATIONAL 8-7117

This FBI poster was issued on June 29, 1964, shortly after civil rights workers Andrew Goodman, James Chaney, and Michael Schwerner went missing. The signature of FBI Director J. Edgar Hoover appears on the poster, despite Hoover's longtime belief that civil rights leaders were a threat to the nation. Pressure by President Lyndon Johnson on Hoover led the FBI to open a field office in Jackson, Mississippi, following the disappearance of the three workers.

SETTING UP THE NEW FIELD OFFICE

The new Jackson, Mississippi, field office had to be set up in a hurry. Roy Moore, the special agent in charge, arrived on July 5, 1964. Hoover was due to arrive five days later to officially open the office. Moore had to have something in place for the director to see. Moore scrambled to find office space on the top floors of a new bank building. Then he moved quickly to get furniture, phones, and other essential equipment. Meanwhile, more than 150 agents were streaming into Jackson.

These agents were not assigned. They had to volunteer. Everyone knew that the work would be very demanding. It would require long hours through burning summer heat—and danger. In addition, civil rights work was not then a high priority for the Bureau. Going to Jackson would not help an agent's career. Still, many were eager to be assigned to the new office.

The discovery of the burned-out car of missing civil rights workers Schwerner, Chaney, and Goodman increased the FBI's fears that they would not be found alive.

state. The interviews they carried out were not always productive. Sullivan, talking to a historian years later, explained why:

Fear of the Klan overlay the uncooperative attitude of some. Others perceived that the civil rights workers were outside troublemakers who had received their just dues.

Despite these barriers, FBI agents continued to probe. They talked to hundreds of people. They looked for physical clues. That meant slogging through swamps full of poisonous rattlesnakes. They tramped through woods. One search uncovered the car that Schwerner, Goodman, and Chaney had been driving. It was burned. That discovery made it even more likely that the civil rights workers had been murdered.

In early August, the FBI got a tip. An **informant** told agents where the bodies of Schwerner, Goodman, and Chaney could be found. The agents paid $30,000 for this information. Sullivan's team began digging into a dam made of packed earth. Inside it they found the bodies of the three civil rights workers. They had been shot and killed.

Mystery Unraveled

Now the FBI had a murder investigation on its hands. The Bureau kept pushing to find out who had done it. Then agent John L. Martin got a break. While interviewing a man named Delmar Dennis, he sensed that Dennis knew something about the crime. Over the course of several meetings, Martin gained Dennis' trust, and coaxed him to agree that the three men should not have been murdered. And then, feeling that Dennis was ready to speak, he tried a tougher approach:

FAST FACTS

During the MIBURN investigation, 258 FBI agents interviewed more than 1,000 people, 480 of whom were members of the Klan. The investigation cost more than $800,000.

I . . . assure you that we are not going to leave Mississippi until we solve the crime. There are two ways for you to go. You can be a **defendant** or you can be a witness. Which is it?

Martin convinced Dennis to talk to men who had been involved in the crime and to get them to give him information about what had happened. Finally, the FBI pieced together its case. They discovered that while the three civil rights workers were being detained by police, a deputy sheriff had told local Klan members that the men would be released. As the three drove off, Klan members in cars—including the deputy sheriff—chased them. Eventually, the Klan members

forced Schwerner, Goodman, and Chaney to stop. They shot the three, burned their car, and buried their bodies to hide the evidence.

The murderers were sure they would remain free. Even if the bodies were found, no jury was likely to find them guilty. African Americans could not serve on juries in Mississippi, and an all-white jury would never convict them of the crime, they believed.

State and Federal Charges

The FBI investigation continued for weeks. Finally, on December 4, 1964, agents arrested 19 men on **federal** charges of conspiring to deprive the three murdered workers of their civil rights. By then, the U.S. government had realized that Mississippi authorities had no intention of bringing charges against anyone who had actually planned or carried out the murders. One of those charged was the county sheriff. Another was the deputy sheriff. In January 1965, all 19 men were formally charged with **conspiracy** in the deaths of Schwerner, Goodman, and Chaney.

In October 1967, after years of legal **appeals** and haggling, seven of the men were found guilty. The deputy sheriff and five others were sentenced to three to 10 years in prison. The head of the local Klan, who had ordered the murders, got 10 years. Testimony from FBI informants was crucial to winning these convictions. Sheriff Lawrence Rainey was one of the 10 men found not guilty.

CHAPTER 2 Reluctant Investigators, Tough Cases, and COINTELPRO

In 1965—less than a year after the murders of Schwerner, Goodman, and Chaney—the FBI faced another civil rights murder. This one occurred in Alabama, where civil rights activists held a drive to register African-American voters. The drive ended with a massive march of thousands of

This photo shows a small portion of the crowd of thousands who marched from Selma to Montgomery, Alabama, in a drive to register African-American voters in March 1965.

The murder of Viola Liuzzo once again focused the attention of the FBI on violence against members of the civil rights movement during the 1960s. The Detroit civil rights activist was killed by a group of Klansmen after participating in the march from Selma to Montgomery in March 1965.

people from Selma to the state capital in Montgomery. On March 25, the last night of the march, workers drove marchers back to their homes in Selma. One of those drivers was Viola Liuzzo. A housewife from Detroit, she had been inspired by the calls for racial justice to help the civil rights movement. As she drove toward Selma that night, another car pulled alongside hers. There were four Ku Klux Klan members inside. One of them shot her in the head. She died instantly.

Instant Outrage—and Results

President Lyndon Johnson was outraged by the attack. He told J. Edgar Hoover to "find the perpetrators of this heinous [monstrous] crime." It took the Bureau no more than a day to solve the murder. On March 26, Johnson held a press conference. With Hoover standing by, the president announced that the Bureau had arrested four members of the Klan for Liuzzo's murder.

How did the FBI solve Liuzzo's murder so quickly? The FBI had an advantage in the case. Gary Thomas Rowe, an FBI informer—and Klan member—was in the car that carried the murderer. Neither Johnson nor Hoover said anything about *how* the FBI broke the case. Years later, in the 1970s, information emerged concerning Rowe's involvement in several racially motivated acts of violence, including the shooting of Viola Liuzzo. It could not be legally proven that Rowe had participated in the shooting or could have prevented it—or that the FBI could be held liable for the attack. The U.S. Justice Department did determine, however, that he had participated in attacks on African Americans, civil rights workers, and reporters. The FBI was criticized for having under its supervision a man with a history of committing violent acts against blacks and members of the civil rights movement. On March 26, 1965, though, Hoover and his men looked brilliant.

The FBI's work in the Schwerner, Goodman, and Chaney murders and the Liuzzo case marked a change of course from its many years of staying away from civil rights cases. Now the Bureau would be more active in these matters.

Early FBI Actions Against Extremists

From the FBI's beginnings as the Bureau of Investigation in 1908, civil rights cases were not part of the Bureau's mission. This was true even though dozens of African Americans were lynched—illegally hanged by mobs—each year. **Lynching** violated federal laws that had been passed in the 1860s to guarantee the civil rights of blacks. But the Bureau refused to act on these cases. In a 1910 report, the Justice Department said it had "no authority . . . to protect citizens of African descent in the enjoyment of civil rights."

During the 1920s, though, the Bureau did help the cause of civil rights in a way. It played a role in the decline of the

THE STATE OF CIVIL RIGHTS AFTER THE CIVIL WAR

In matters of civil rights, especially under the leadership of J. Edgar Hoover, who served as director of the FBI between 1924 and 1972, the FBI often reflected national laws, practices, and attitudes toward civil rights. Not all of those attitudes were positive, and from the earliest days in its history, the FBI had been slow to act on civil rights cases.

In the decades following the Civil War, the U.S. Congress passed civil rights laws that guaranteed freedoms to African Americans following the abolition of slavery. Despite these laws, however, African Americans and other minority communities suffered from discrimination. Laws known as Jim Crow laws allowed for certain types of segregation—the separation of people based on race. In the nation as a whole, for example, the U.S. military and most professional sports were segregated until during or after World War II.

In the South, Jim Crow laws were particularly harsh and pervasive. There, states passed laws that denied people their voting and other civil rights. State laws in the South also segregated everything from drinking fountains, restaurants, public transportation, and movie theaters to schools, medical facilities, and membership in certain trades. The civil rights movement struggled to overturn these laws and reverse the feelings that had long fueled them. The movement achieved major successes with the passage of various civil rights acts into law in the 1950s and 1960s.

At right, a man drinks from a water fountain designated for black males. During the 1960s, civil rights activists lobbied to end the segregation of public facilities in the South.

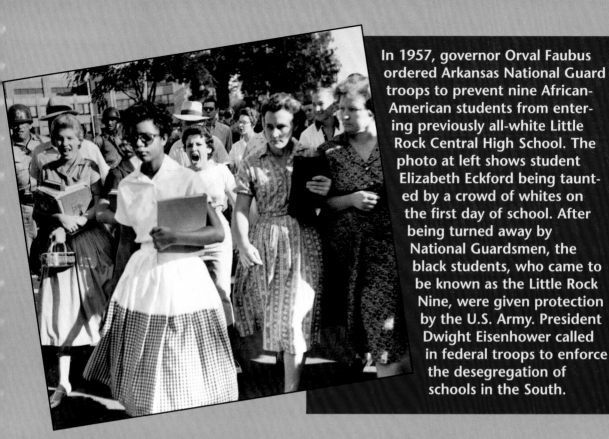

In 1957, governor Orval Faubus ordered Arkansas National Guard troops to prevent nine African-American students from entering previously all-white Little Rock Central High School. The photo at left shows student Elizabeth Eckford being taunted by a crowd of whites on the first day of school. After being turned away by National Guardsmen, the black students, who came to be known as the Little Rock Nine, were given protection by the U.S. Army. President Dwight Eisenhower called in federal troops to enforce the desegregation of schools in the South.

In the North, blacks were more likely to be legally entitled to use the same facilities, ride the same buses, go to the same hospitals and schools, and live in the same neighborhoods as whites. But many businesses, institutions, and individuals in the North practiced a more subtle form of discrimination. As a result of this type of segregation, known as *de facto* segregation, African Americans were likely to be discriminated against when they tried to move into neighborhoods and attend schools that were primarily white.

Blacks in the North—particularly in the larger cities to which many had moved after the Civil War—found themselves victimized not so much by the laws of the states in which they lived but by the attitudes of whites who could not be forced to sell or rent property to them or hire them to work in their businesses. As a result, many African Americans in the North found themselves living in segregated neighborhoods, attending schools that were entirely or mostly black, and struggling to find employment in businesses that were owned by whites. The quality of their homes, schools, and livelihoods suffered, with substandard housing, poor education, and grinding poverty an outcome that took root over many decades and persists to this day.

Ku Klux Klan. By the 1910s, the Klan was rising in power and influence. Membership grew, and in many states, Klan members held elected offices. As Klan membership grew, violence spread. Louisiana's governor, John M. Parker, grew desperate. He wrote an appeal to the Bureau of Investigation:

> Men have been taken out and whipped. Two men have been murdered. These conditions are beyond the control of the state.

The Bureau found evidence that resulted in charges being brought against several Louisiana law enforcement officers. But these men were tried in state court by juries that included Klan members. The juries would not convict them.

The Bureau then took a new approach. One Klan leader, Edward Y. Clarke, was traveling from state to state as part of his Klan activities. On these trips, he brought with him an unmarried woman named Laurel Martin. That made him vulnerable. A federal law known as the Mann Act made it illegal to take women or girls across state lines for immoral purposes. The Mann Act was primarily intended to enforce laws against **prostitution**, which was called "white slavery" at the time, but it could be applied to other types of behavior deemed immoral. Enforcement of the Mann Act was well within the **jurisdiction** of the Bureau, which used it as a way of bringing federal charges against Clarke. In 1923, Bureau agents arrested Clarke for breaking this law.

Clarke pleaded guilty in 1924 to the charges issued against him. The incident broke his power. He had claimed that the Klan promoted morality, but his own crime made that claim seem absurd. Other Klan leaders were also found to have engaged in crimes or other immoral acts. With many leaders shamed, the Klan lost members, and its power in the South declined.

Hoover and Civil Rights

For the next few decades, the FBI focused on catching gangsters and finding communists. During the 1950s, though, civil rights protests began to sweep across the South. Sometimes, local police departments used violence against protestors. In 1956, President Dwight Eisenhower asked Hoover whether the FBI should become more involved in civil rights work. Hoover said no. He gave several reasons:

- The most important white political and economic leaders in the South favor segregation.
- Communists have a major influence in civil rights groups.
- The Ku Klux Klan, the main group of white extremists, has little power.
- The FBI does not have the manpower or budget for such work.

A group of Klansmen march through Washington, D.C., in this photo from the 1920s. Despite the Klan's history of violence against African Americans, Jews, and other minorities, the FBI long held that the group had little power. That stance changed in the 1960s when civil rights workers were murdered in the South.

FAST FACTS

Facts did not support Hoover's claim that communists were linked to the civil rights movement. In the 1950s, the FBI found fewer than 500 past or present communists who belonged to the National Association for the Advancement of Colored People (NAACP), a major civil rights group. At the time, the NAACP had more than 300,000 members.

Hoover might have believed those statements to be true. He had other reasons not to be active in civil rights cases, though. First, Hoover himself believed that whites and African Americans should be kept separate. Second, he did not want to upset white southerners. He knew the power and influence of the Bureau depended on keeping them happy. Many southern members of Congress had great influence on how much money the Bureau received each year. If the FBI pursued civil rights cases, Hoover believed that politicians from the South would cut the FBI's budget. Also, pushing civil rights cases would anger southern police. They would become less willing to work closely with the FBI, reducing the Bureau's ability to solve other types of crimes.

The Evers Case

Under Hoover's leadership, the FBI did little about civil rights cases until 1963. That year, a white extremist shot and killed Medgar Evers in Jackson, Mississippi. Evers, an African American, had been a civil rights leader in the state.

FBI agents found the gun that had been used in the murder. Using finger-prints on the gun, the FBI identified a white extremist named Byron De La Beckwith as Evers's killer. Beckwith was tried twice in 1964 for murder in state courts. Both times, all-white juries were unable to find him guilty.

Mourners are shown marching through Jackson, Mississippi, in 1963 during a funeral procession honoring slain civil rights leader Medgar Evers. Among the mourners was Martin Luther King, Jr. (second row, first on left). In 1968, King would also be slain.

Going After the Klan

The year after the Evers murder came the MIBURN investigation. That same summer, President Johnson pushed Hoover on another matter. By 1964, the Klan had grown larger and more violent. At a White House meeting, Johnson said to Hoover:

> Edgar, I want you to put people after the Klan and study it from one county to the next. I want the FBI to have the best **intelligence** system possible to check on the activities of these people.

Hoover followed the president's orders. In June, he ordered a COINTELPRO—a **counterintelligence** program—aimed at the Ku Klux Klan. The FBI had carried out a similar program against the Communist Party in 1956. The program had included placing **wiretaps** on the phones of party members so their conversations could be heard. It also involved FBI agents turning party members into informants so that the FBI could know the group's plans. Now Hoover planned to use similar techniques against more than a dozen Klan groups and nine other hate groups, including the American Nazi Party. Once pushed to act, the Bureau moved quickly. In a little less than a year, the FBI had more than 2,000 informants.

The FBI used several methods to fight the Klan. First, it used informants such as Gary Thomas Rowe to name members responsible for attacks and murders. Second, it used harassment. It secretly investigated Klan leaders, hoping to find information that would put them in a bad light. The

Bureau also gave reporters and writers information that presented the Klan in a bad light—and made the Bureau look good for fighting Klan crimes.

Over the next few years, the Klan lost power. In 1964, the Klan had about 14,000 members. By 1971, membership had dropped to about 4,000. Violence fell also.

The FBI COINTELPRO was hardly the only reason that the Klan lost power. Congress passed new laws that guaranteed equal rights for blacks. Southern political leaders worked to stop violence. Many ordinary southern whites realized that the time had come for more just treatment of African Americans, and they worked for change. Still, the FBI deserves credit for helping to end the Klan's terror.

The Cold Case Initiative

Although the violence of the civil rights era ended as the Klan's influence declined, many who committed violent crimes were not immediately punished. In some cases, FBI agents had gathered evidence linking southern whites to attacks on African Americans. Often, though, state officials refused to bring charges. Other crimes were never even investigated.

In the 1990s, changes began. Prosecuting attorneys in the South began reviving some of the old cases. In 1994, a Mississippi prosecutor brought new charges against Byron De La Beckwith, the man believed to have killed Medgar Evers. At this trial, the prosecutor presented the FBI's original evidence along with important new evidence. This time, the jury found Beckwith guilty of the murder. Other revived cases followed. In 2005, Edgar Ray Killen—one of the men who had killed Schwerner, Goodman, and Chaney—was convicted of

In 2005, more than 40 years after the murders of Michael Schwerner, Andrew Goodman, and James Chaney, Edgar Ray Killen (shown top left in 1964) was found guilty of new charges issued against him. Schwerner's wife Rita is shown at a voter-registration training session just before her husband's death in 1964 (top right) and (right) speaking with Chaney's brother Ben during a recess in Killen's trial in 2005.

manslaughter and sentenced to 60 years in prison.

In 2006, a letter was sent to the FBI's Atlanta field office asking about the unsolved murder of two African-American men in 1964. The letter prompted the FBI to ask all its field offices to list cases that were unsolved or had never been prosecuted. The next year, FBI Director Robert S. Mueller announced an effort by the Bureau to pursue about 100 of these "cold cases." Mueller said, "Protecting the civil rights of all Americans is one of the FBI's highest missions, whether the violations occurred four days ago or 40 years ago."

3 The Darker Story

Although J. Edgar Hoover moved against the Klan—when he was ordered to do so—he had little sympathy for the civil rights movement. Early in the 1960s, his agents did little to help solve civil rights crimes. At the same time, the Bureau did not act to prevent violence against civil rights workers. As activist Andrew Young later told a historian, "No matter what kind of brutality [took place], all the FBI agents did was stand over on the corner and take notes." This hands-off approach stirred resentment among civil rights workers.

Civil rights leader Martin Luther King, Jr. (front row, second from right), leads a five-day, 50-mile (80-kilometer) march from Selma, Alabama, to the state capitol at Montgomery in March 1965 to protest the lack of voting rights for African Americans. Until the mid-1960s, the FBI had done little to protect members of the civil rights movement against violence—or even to solve civil rights crimes once they were committed.

A Waste of Resources

At the same time that the Bureau was cracking down on the Ku Klux Klan, Hoover also directed the FBI to investigate the civil rights movement. The FBI director firmly believed that communists were supporting and controlling the civil rights movement. He insisted that FBI agents search for these connections. That effort turned out to be a waste of the Bureau's resources. So, too, was the FBI's harassment of Martin Luther King, Jr., the best-known leader of the civil rights movement. Hoover believed that King was dangerous. He directed FBI agents to find information that could be used to make King look bad.

Finally, the FBI carried out a COINTELPRO aimed at African-American organizations. Some of these, such as the Black Panther Party, were militant groups that used threats and violence to achieve their goals. However, other groups on which the FBI spied were non-violent, such as the NAACP and the Congress of Racial Equality (CORE). Some of the steps that the Bureau took, such as wiretapping and other forms of spying, pushed past the limits of the law.

The Voting Rights Probe

When John F. Kennedy became president in 1961, new officials moved into the Department of Justice. Two of them, Burke Marshall and John Doar, hoped to break the hold of whites on state governments in the South. They wanted to bring lawsuits charging state officials with denying African Americans the right to register to vote. To sue, they needed evidence. Marshall and Doar hoped to use FBI agents to gather that evidence, but Hoover was reluctant to become involved. He told his agents to drag their feet.

The FBI agents did an incomplete job. They did gather evidence related to illegally denying African Americans the right to vote, but they did nothing to analyze it. The Justice Department lawyers would have to do that work.

This action was unusual for the Bureau, which historically took great pride in its ability to gather information and then to put it to use to investigate wrongdoing and solve crimes. Marshall and Doar tried to push Hoover to cooperate and help the Justice Department prosecute people who were found to be breaking the law in matters related to voting rights. They ordered him to have his agents interview African Americans and whites in the

Members of the Black Panther Party call for the release of their controversial leader, Huey Newton, in July 1968. Newton faced charges in the killing of an Oakland, California, police officer during a gun battle. Known for both their community-service programs and sometimes violent encounters with the law, the Panthers were targeted by the FBI's COINTELPRO through spying and infiltration of its membership.

South. Hoover went along, but again he gave agents directions that limited the usefulness of the interviews. In the end, Doar sent his own lawyers south to do the interviews. Bogged down by work the FBI had not done, the Justice Department could not bring as many lawsuits as had been hoped. Hoover had succeeded in blocking the effort to gain voting rights for African Americans.

Standing Aside

Another problem with FBI attitudes and behavior toward the civil rights movement was its refusal to protect activists. Civil rights workers willingly risked their lives in pursuing their cause. Dozens were killed, and hundreds more were brutally beaten. Whether the attacks were made by Klan members or police officers, the FBI did nothing.

The Bureau claimed that its role was to investigate crimes—not to act as bodyguards. Still, FBI agents could have stepped in and arrested the attackers. Beating someone engaged in a nonviolent protest is a clear violation of civil rights. Under orders from headquarters, however, agents usually just watched.

The FBI also ignored its responsibility to investigate many attacks. John Doar received an FBI report on five attacks that took place in Mississippi in 1961. The report left out many important details about how badly the civil rights activists were hurt.

Doar was stunned when he received another report sent by one of the attacked workers. It revealed far more serious injuries than the FBI had stated. Shocked, he ordered agents back into the field to do their jobs better.

U.S. Attorney John Doar (center) is shown confronting Mississippi Lieutenant Governor Paul Johnson (left) in 1962. Johnson was attempting to block James Meredith (right), the first African American to be enrolled in the University of Mississippi, from entering the campus. Doar was considered by many to be a hero of the civil rights movement. He championed voting rights legislation and prosecuted those responsible for killing civil rights workers in the 1960s. He also worked at getting the FBI to become more responsive in gathering evidence in civil rights cases.

The Supposed Communist Connection

Hoover's unwillingness to help investigate and charge those responsible for denying blacks their voting rights was not softened by his mistaken belief concerning supposed communist influence within the civil rights movement. He maintained this belief despite the fact that his agents could never prove such a link. He ordered a probe called COMINFIL (short for "communist infiltration") in October 1962. It was aimed at finding communists among the people associated with Martin Luther King, Jr. Agents did find that two of King's associates had had ties with the Communist Party USA. But wiretaps on these men's phones never produced any evidence that they were actively involved in the party or that any associations they may have had with communism played a role in their role in the civil rights movement. Other intelligence revealed no strong connection between communists and the civil rights movement in general.

In 1963, a top FBI official tried to argue this point with Hoover. William C. Sullivan headed up the FBI's Domestic Intelligence Division (DID). In September 1963, Sullivan wrote a 70-page memo saying that communists could not be found in the civil rights movement.

Hoover rebuked Sullivan and his report. On his copy of the report, he wrote a scathing note showing his displeasure with the conclusion and his insistence on a connection between the civil rights movement and the Communist Party. Sullivan backed down.

William C. Sullivan, of the FBI's Domestic Intelligence Division (DID), testifies before the President's Commission on Campus Unrest in 1970. In 1963, Sullivan had briefly argued against FBI Director J. Edgar Hoover's claim that the civil rights movement was infiltrated by communists. When Hoover blasted Sullivan's report, Sullivan backed down from his claims. In a remarkable about-face, he then advocated a domestic **surveillance** program aimed at discrediting civil rights leader Martin Luther King, Jr.

In another memo Sullivan wrote, "The Director is correct. We were completely wrong . . . the Communist Party, USA, does wield substantial influence over Negroes [African Americans] which one day could become decisive."

FAST FACTS

The FBI gathered huge amounts of data on Martin Luther King, Jr. Headquarters in Washington had at least 200,000 pages. Field offices had as many as 500,000 more. One scholar thinks that the total may be closer to 1 million pages of data on King.

Sullivan had every reason to back down. He was afraid for his job—and for the jobs of the agents who worked with him in DID. If he continued to disagree with Hoover, his future in the Bureau would not be bright. Sullivan responded by offering a new plan that was even more extreme than COMINFIL.

The FBI Goes After King

Sullivan proposed an organized plan to carry out surveillance on Martin Luther King, Jr. He called King the "most dangerous Negro . . . from the standpoint of Communism, the Negro, and national security." The goal was to find information that could be made public so that King would lose influence. In the fall of 1963, the Bureau asked Attorney General Robert F. Kennedy to approve placing a wiretap in King's home. Kennedy approved the wiretap.

The Bureau went even farther. Over the years—without Kennedy's knowledge—it placed microphones in hotel rooms where King stayed during his travels across the country.

FBI agents listened to

The FBI was not the only organization that embarked on a crusade to discredit the civil rights movement and its leaders, particularly Martin Luther King, Jr. Sadly, its efforts played into the hands of extremist groups that used tactics such as this billboard, placed on highways in 1965, which purports to show King at a "communist training school."

King's phone calls and conversations. They listened whether the conversations were about plans for civil rights actions or personal matters. During the hours of tapes, agents recorded some embarrassing personal information. Then, each time King received an honor or an award, the FBI gave reporters information aimed at ruining his reputation.

Sometimes the FBI went even farther. In the fall of 1964, the DID made a fake tape that supposedly had evidence that King was involved with women other than his wife. The FBI then sent the tape to King for him and his wife to hear. The package came with a note that threatened to make the tape public. That step was never taken, and the action eventually came to reflect more poorly on the FBI than on King.

Hoover and King had several public arguments. King criticized the FBI several times for not doing enough to aid the civil rights movement. Hoover, in 1964, responded harshly. That November, at a press conference, he called King the "most notorious liar in the country."

The FBI's watch on King lasted five years, until his death. The surveillance did not become known until the 1970s, after both King and Hoover were dead. The news tarnished the FBI's reputation. Members of Congress who held hearings on the matter criticized the Bureau's actions.

Targeting the Black Panthers and Others

In the middle to the late 1960s, some African Americans took a new approach to the struggle for rights. King and other

BREAKING THE RULES

J. Edgar Hoover said that the FBI had no authority to become involved in civil rights matters. When it suited him, though, he used the Bureau to do whatever he wanted.

In 1964, a group of African Americans and their supporters from Mississippi formed the Mississippi Freedom Democratic Party (MFDP). They meant to challenge the regular Democratic Party in the state because the regular Democrats were blocking the civil rights movement. This plan created a problem for the national Democratic Party, which that August would hold its convention to nominate a candidate for president. It would pick President Lyndon Johnson as its nominee. Johnson did not want any embarrassing scenes, however. He worried that the MFDP might stage protests.

The president asked the FBI to carry out surveillance of the MFDP. Hoover agreed. Agents placed wiretaps in MFDP offices and hotel rooms. Some agents posed as reporters to get information that way. Whatever they learned was quickly sent back to FBI headquarters and from there to the White House. The whole operation was completely outside the lines of what the FBI was authorized to do, but it was also typical of the lengths to which the Bureau was willing to go under J. Edgar Hoover to collect damaging information on civil rights leaders.

leaders had preached nonviolent protest. Now, some younger African Americans called for resistance to the racism that blacks faced—in some cases, to the point of advocating armed struggle. These groups tended to be small. Their views alarmed many people, though—including J. Edgar Hoover. Hoover called one of these groups, the Black Panther Party, "the greatest threat to the internal security of the country."

In August 1967, Hoover approved a COINTELPRO operation aimed at "black nationalist hate groups." Black nationalists took the struggle for civil rights a step further, advocating various degrees of black independence from mainstream white America. Some groups were more militant than others. Only the most extreme might be called "hate groups" in the sense of preaching violence against whites. Interestingly, the groups targeted by Hoover's FBI included several nonviolent groups, such as King's Southern Christian Leadership Conference. But the Black Panthers and other more extreme groups were also targets.

The COINTELPRO lasted several years. As with other similar operations, some FBI actions were aimed at harassing Panther leaders. Agents spread rumors about them to discredit them. They also infiltrated the Panthers and other radical black groups to create conflict among the leaders of the Panthers and between the Panthers and other groups.

In some cases, the FBI went beyond the law to carry out its objectives against black militants. On December 4, 1969, an FBI informant gave information that Chicago police officers used to enter an apartment where Black Panther leader Fred Hampton was staying and kill him. The police claimed they had fired in self-defense, but it was determined afterwards that the informant had drugged Hampton's meal earlier to be sure he was asleep when the police raided the apartment. Also, according to eyewitnesses and evidence found at the apartment, the police fired dozens of bullets.

Mark Clark, a Panther who had a gun with him when the police broke in, managed to get off a shot before he was killed by the police. His shot was the only one fired by any of the Panthers in the apartment. No charges were issued against anyone who had planned or conducted the raid. Later, the families of Hampton and Clark filed a lawsuit for nearly $48 million charging that the victims' civil rights had been violated. In 1982, more than 10 years after the suit had been filed, the federal government agreed to settle the suit by paying the families $1.85 million.

By the mid-1970s, the Black Panther Party had few members and little power. What survived the party's decline, however, was recognition of the FBI's COINTELPRO against it—as a dark page in the history of the Bureau.

Black Panther leader Eldridge Cleaver, candidate for president on the Peace and Freedom Party ticket in 1968, is shown standing beside a bullet-riddled campaign poster in the window of Black Panther headquarters in Oakland, California. Although no one was injured, Oakland law enforcement officers were implicated in the shooting.

4 The FBI and Civil Rights Today: Hate Crimes

"Remember 9/11," the note said. Then it took a more frightening turn: "You and your kids will pay."

A Muslim-American woman had received the note, and it frightened her. The date "9/11" referred to the terrorist attacks of September 11, 2001. In those attacks, Muslim terrorists hijacked four planes, flew three of them into important buildings in New York City and Washington, D.C., and, after struggling for control of the plane with passengers and crew members, crashed the

The terrorist attacks of September 11, 2001, including the flying of two passenger jets into the World Trade Center (right), spawned a rash of threats and violence directed against Muslims. These and other **hate crimes** are investigated by the FBI as specific threats against people's civil rights.

fourth into a field in Pennsylvania. About 3,000 people died in those attacks. The woman feared what the person who wrote the note might have in mind for her and her children. At first, she hesitated to tell anyone. Eventually, though, she contacted the FBI field office in Philadelphia.

The FBI analyzed the note for clues about its sender. The message in the note was made by pasting together words cut out of printed pages. FBI agents found that the type in the note matched the type in some brochures found at the hotel where the woman worked. This discovery suggested that the sender of the note worked there, too.

FBI agents narrowed the search by questioning workers at the hotel. A few months later, a hotel employee was charged with making and sending the threatening note. That act broke a federal law that makes it illegal to threaten people because of their race, ethnic origin, religion, or other characteristics.

The FBI and Hate Crimes

The threat to the Muslim-American hotel worker is a hate crime. Federal law defines these crimes as actions "against a person or property motivated in whole or in part by an offender's bias against a race, religion, disability, ethnic origin or sexual orientation." Hate crimes are one of the main areas that are the focus of FBI civil rights work today. Hate crimes include such actions as assault—attacking some-one—or vandalism—destroying a person's property. As the case about the note to the Muslim-American woman shows, simply the threat of violence may be considered a hate crime. In all these cases, the attack or the threat must occur because the victim belongs to a particular category.

The FBI is the only agency of the federal government with the authority to investigate civil rights crimes. That includes hate crimes. Most hate crimes are investigated by state and local law officers and **prosecuted** under state laws. Still, the FBI can help these groups. The groups can call on the FBI crime lab and on FBI workers who

FAST FACTS

The number of hate-crime incidents has dropped in recent years. The number reached a peak in 2001, when 9,730 took place. In 2007, there were only 7,624 incidents, which was a decrease of nearly a hundred from the previous year.

are highly skilled in analyzing technical information. Some FBI agents are experts in determining whether a crime has a hate-based motivation.

The FBI began keeping statistics on hate crimes in 1991. In 2007, the FBI reported 7,624 separate incidents that involved more than 9,000 hate crimes. (Each incident can involve more than one crime.) More than half of the hate crimes—5,408—were crimes against people. Nearly half of those crimes against people were threats. Nine of the crimes were murders.

The other hate crimes—3,579 of them—were property crimes. Four out of every five of those property crimes involved vandalism.

More than half of the hate crimes were motivated by racial or ethnic bias. Since the terrorist attacks of September 11, 2001, hate crimes against Muslims have been on the rise.

Organizing Against Hate Crimes

The FBI uses several different approaches in the fight against hate crimes. One important part of the FBI's work is to teach and train local law enforcement officials about these crimes. The FBI uses two approaches:

Hate Crimes Working Groups (HCWGs). Back in 1998, the FBI worked with other parts of the Justice Department to write a program for teaching law enforcement officers to spot and investigate hate crimes. FBI field offices have HCWGs that continue to work with local law enforcement agencies to find ways to solve hate crimes.

Training Sessions. Each year, the FBI holds hundreds of training programs on hate crimes. These programs are aimed at law enforcement officials. They also include religious groups and organizations with minority groups as members.

The 1990s saw a rising number of cases in which churches with African-American members were set on fire. In 1996, the government set up a National Church Arson Task Force. (The crime of deliberately starting a fire is called arson.) The FBI takes part in this task force.

The FBI also works with national groups such as the National Organization for Women and the Southern Poverty Law Center. The FBI's goal in this effort is to set

THE TRAVELING TRUNK

One way that the FBI works against hate crimes is to teach about them. The Knoxville, Tennessee, field office belongs to a group called the East Tennessee Civil Rights Working Group. That group has put together an exhibit called "The Traveling Trunk." The trunk contains objects that symbolize prejudice and hate crimes. These objects include the following, some of which are pictured in the photo below:

- A Ku Klux Klan robe.
- A charred cross.
- Leg shackles used on slaves.
- A piece of the federal office building in Oklahoma City that was bombed by domestic terrorists.
- Objects from the Holocaust, in which millions of Jews and other minorities were enslaved and murdered by Nazi Germany during World War II.
- Bandanas worn by members of street gangs.
- Photographs of hate crimes.
- Wreckage from the World Trade Center, which was destroyed in the September 11, 2001, attacks.
- Muslim clothing, which symbolizes a group that has become a new target of hate crimes.

A member of the East Tennessee Civil Rights Working Group named Gene Rosenberg thought of the Traveling Trunk. He uses it as a teaching tool. He goes to schools in Tennessee and other states to teach students about hate crimes. These lessons help students see why hate crimes are bad and reexamine their own views toward groups of people who are different. Richard Lambert, the special agent in charge of the Knoxville field office, said this about the Traveling Trunk: "It sends a very powerful message about hate to anyone who sees it, and I think it will have a long-lasting and powerful impact, particularly on students."

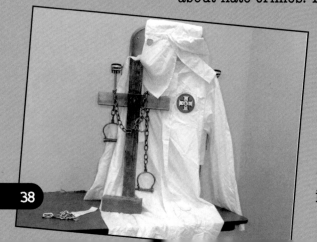

up good relations with the groups so that they and the FBI can share information. Then, if the people served by one of those groups are attacked in a hate crime, the FBI is in a good position to investigate and to help.

Examples of Hate Crimes

An African-American family was looking at a home for sale in northern Florida in 2006. A white man who lived next door put together a large wooden cross in his own yard, covered it with some liquid that would burn, and set it on fire. Then he warned the family's 15-year-old son to tell his parents not to buy the house.

This cross burning was a hate crime. The Ku Klux

This cross was burned in front of Nelson Espinoza's home in Rockfield, Kentucky, in September 2006. Burning crosses have been a symbol of racial and religious intolerance in the United States for decades. A handwritten note, also left on his lawn, reads, "My country, maybe. My neighborhood, NO WAY!!!" Such acts of vandalism reflect anti-immigrant bigotry directed against Latinos, who have become recent targets of hate crimes.

Klan had burned crosses from the 1920s to the 1960s to threaten blacks across the South. This nasty way of delivering a message of hate is now rare, but it does occur. About 20 cross burnings took place from October 2005 to April 2007. The act can frighten its targets—and it can have bad consequences for the person who does it. Neal Chapman Coombs, who burned that cross in Florida, was charged with violating the civil rights of the African-American family he threatened. After pleading guilty, he was sentenced to more than a year in prison.

Defacing property with **anti-Semitic** graffiti, such as these swastikas at a Jewish cemetery in New Jersey, is considered a hate crime because it targets a group on the basis of religion and ethnicity.

Far across the country, in Eugene, Oregon, another hate crime took place. Gabriel and Jacob Laskey and three other men threw rocks through the windows of a Jewish temple. Carved into the rocks were swastikas—the symbols of Nazi Germany in the 1930s and 1940s. During World War II, the Nazis had rounded up and killed more than 6 million European Jews. This incidence of rock throwing was clearly a message of hate.

When they were arrested and charged, the Laskey brothers admitted their guilt. Jacob remained committed to his intolerant beliefs. He was sentenced to more than 10 years in prison for the attack and for related crimes. Gabriel Laskey had a change of heart, however. He apologized for the things he did. He asked a federal judge to suspend his sentence. Because he seemed sincere, the judge granted his wish, although he did place Laskey on five years of **probation**.

CHAPTER 5
The FBI and Civil Rights Today: Color of Law

On August 11, 2006, police in Los Angeles arrested a man they suspected of being a gang member. Two officers were on the scene. They held the man down on the ground to place handcuffs on him. While holding him down, one officer punched the man in the face several times.

A bystander with a cell phone camera recorded the scene and posted it on the Web site YouTube. Over the next few weeks, the video was viewed more than 150,000 times. That might be the end of the story—except that the video

This scene is from a video recording taken on a cell phone and posted on YouTube. It shows a police officer punching a suspected gang member in the face during an arrest in Los Angeles. The video led to an FBI investigation into possible violations of the suspect's civil rights.

led to an FBI investigation. One of the areas of civil rights that the FBI investigates is called "color of law." The phrase refers to actions by government and police officers carrying out their official duties. When they carry out those duties, they must treat all people equally and not take advantage of their power.

The FBI investigation aimed to see whether the police officers used excessive force. If so, they would have broken the "color of law" rules. They could be charged with violating the civil rights of the man they arrested.

Investigating the Powerful

The words "EQUAL JUSTICE UNDER LAW" are engraved on the U.S. Supreme Court building. These are strong words, and they proclaim a basic principle of U.S. government. Each person should be treated in the same way as all others. The goal is to guarantee that everyone who appears in court has a fair trial. This principle also covers the behavior of police officers when they investigate crimes and arrest suspects. It applies to mayors and governors as well. If they claim to be carrying out their official duties, they must be doing so—and they must do so fairly.

The words "EQUAL JUSTICE UNDER LAW" are shown here on the front of the U.S. Supreme Court building. These words, written to apply to equal treatment in a court of law, also stand behind the principle of the "color of law" rule, which aims to guarantee that everyone is treated equally by law enforcement officers.

Color of law crimes involve public officials whose actions violate the civil rights of the victim. The FBI investigates five main kinds of crimes in this area:

- *Too much force*. This was the kind of crime suspected in the case of the Los Angeles police officers that opened this chapter. Police officers sometimes have to use force to subdue a suspect. If they use too much force, though, they might violate that suspect's civil rights.
- *Sexual attacks*. People who are in police custody or in prison are at the mercy of the law enforcement officers guarding them. Sometimes those guards take advantage of their power by forcing a prisoner to have sexual relations with them. Doing so is a civil rights crime under color of law.
- *False arrest or faking of evidence*. Police officers have a duty to be honest in their dealings with suspects. Sometimes, though, officers go beyond the law as they

FAST FACTS

The Department of Justice gets about 10,000 color of law complaints each year. Police officers are the targets of about three-quarters of these complaints. Only about 30 officers are prosecuted each year in federal court, though others may be tried in local or state courts.

seek revenge for some harm or as they try to make sure that a person they suspect is a criminal gets punished. They might arrest a person on false charges and then force that person to confess to another crime. They might also create false evidence linking a person to a crime. These actions violate the victim's civil rights.

- *Taking away someone's property*. Americans can only lose property through "due process of law." People can have their goods or homes taken from them only if they are brought to trial in the courts—and given a fair trial. Any action that uses the power of public office to take away another person's property violates the civil rights of the victim.

- *Failure to protect a person from harm*. Sometimes the public develops strong feelings against a person suspected, or convicted, of a crime. That person might then be under the threat of a violent attack. If public officials do not take steps to protect the person, the

Police arrest a suspected crack dealer in Atlanta, Georgia. Digital and cell-phone video cameras have placed law enforcement officers under greater public scrutiny than ever before as they subdue suspects and make arrests.

officials might be guilty of a crime under color of law.

The Power of Civil Cases

Color of law cases can be either criminal or civil. In a criminal case, the state or federal government charges the official with committing a crime. If the official is found guilty, he or she is sentenced to prison or fined, or both. Criminal charges can be brought for just one incident of abuse of power.

In a civil case, the Department of Justice sues the person who violated the victim's civil rights. It might also sue the agency or department of the government that employs that person if its policies led to the abuse of power. The department does not bring suits over individual acts of abuse of power. FBI investigators must find a "pattern or practice" of misconduct. For instance, a group representing African Americans might complain that state police are more likely to stop black drivers than white drivers. To win this case, the group must prove this pattern of action over a period of time.

MAKING A COLOR OF LAW COMPLAINT

People who believe they are victims of a color of law violation must formally notify the Department of Justice. They can contact an FBI field office or head-quarters or the Civil Rights Division of the Department of Justice.

A complaint has to include basic information about the case. The victim must state his or her name, address, and phone number so investigators can make further contact. Of course, the person or agency of the government being accused also has to be named. In addition, the complaint must include details about the reasons for the complaint. It has to list the dates on which problems occurred and where they took place. The complaint has to describe what happened in detail. If the victim suffered any injuries, those should be spelled out.

Rodney King (right), shown here with his attorney on May 1, 1992, makes a statement in which he pleads for an end to rioting in South Central Los Angeles. When four white police officers were declared innocent in the beating of King during a traffic stop, Los Angeles erupted in one of the deadliest riots of the 20th century. Three days after the April 29 verdict, 55 people were dead and more than 2,000 were injured. Following that trial, which took place in state court, the U.S. Department of Justice filed its own charges in federal court. Two of the four officers were subsequently found guilty on charges related to civil rights law, and two were acquitted.

If the Department of Justice wins the suit, the government body that lost must change its practices to end the unfairness. For instance, a police department must take steps to prevent officers from using too much force. In some cases, the victim can also sue. If he or she wins, the government agency might have to pay a sum of money as damages.

Sample Cases

Perhaps the most famous color of law case is the beating of an African-American man named Rodney King in Los Angeles in 1991. King was stopped by Los Angeles police officers on a traffic violation. When he ran from them, they chased after him. When the officers caught King, they beat him many times with their nightsticks.

The officers were tried in state court for using too much force. The jury found them not guilty. After that decision, the Department of Justice sued the officers for violating King's civil rights. One of the four, Sergeant Stacy Koon, claimed he should be dropped from the case. He said that he had merely watched the beating and not taken part in it. The trial judge ruled that the officer should not be dropped from the case. The judge said that by not acting, Koon also had "subject[ed] the victim to the loss of his or her right to be kept free from harm while in official custody." In the end, Koon and one of the officers who had hit King were found guilty of breaking the law. The other two were acquitted.

A prison incident in 2006 raised the question of officials not acting to protect someone in their custody. In September of that year, an inmate in a California prison was beaten to death by other inmates. The killing was investigated, but no charges were made. Later, however, new information emerged, and the FBI resumed its investigation.

According to these new findings, prison guards were not patrolling the cells but were relaxing, watching television and playing cards. Also, they had put in place a system in which some prisoners were given the task of disciplining other prisoners when rules were broken. That system might have led to the prisoner's death. If so, it was a matter of "pattern and practice"—the kind of ongoing behavior that breaks civil rights law.

CHAPTER 6
The FBI and Civil Rights Today: Human Trafficking

In 1999, a 14-year-old girl was taken from an orphanage in Haiti. She was given fake immigration papers and sent to Miami, Florida. She had no knowledge of what would happen to her.

For the next six years, the teen was forced to work in the home of a Miami couple as a servant. Actually, she was a

Several cargo ships piled high with containers are shown docked in a port, ready to be unloaded. These containers are intended to be used to carry large shipments of products to and from overseas ports. Often, however, their cargo consists of people who have paid large sums of money to be transported illegally into the United States. In some cases, people are packed so tightly and the conditions are so terrible that many do not survive the voyage.

slave. Seven days a week, up to 15 hours a day, she cooked, cleaned, and gardened. She was never paid. If she refused to work, she was beaten. At times, the couple threatened to hand the girl over to the police or to send her back to Haiti.

Finally, in June 2005, a friend of the couple helped the victim escape. Eventually, her situation came to the attention of the FBI. Agents investigated and gave their findings to prosecutors. In 2008, three people were found guilty of violating the girl's civil rights, forcing her to engage in forced labor, and sheltering an illegal immigrant. One of them was sentenced to more than seven years in prison. She also had to pay more than $160,000 to the victim.

A Department of Justice official thanked the victim for making the crime known. Said Acting Assistant Attorney General Grace Chung Becker:

> I applaud the courage of the victim in this case, who made this prosecution possible. The Department of Justice is committed to work vigorously to end this type of forced servitude.

Florencia Molina, shown here in September 2005, was a victim of human trafficking. Virtually enslaved at a Los Angeles dressmaking shop, she worked up to 17 hours a day, seven days a week. She also lived there, forced to share a small bed in a storage closet with another woman from Mexico and not allowed to shower or wash her clothes.

What Is Human Trafficking?

Human trafficking is the crime of buying and selling people and their work. "Trafficking" is part of the name because the victims are moved from one place to another. Often they are taken from their homes. Sometimes, though, they are young people who have run away from home. Some of these run-aways fall into the hands of criminals who trick them. The criminals may promise a better life in a new city or country. In the end, though, they treat their victims as slaves.

Commenting on busting up one trafficking ring, Special Agent Robert Schoch described the problem:

> These young women were enticed into coming to this country by promises of the American dream, only to arrive and discover that what awaited was a nightmare.

In many cases, the criminals get their young victims addicted to drugs. Once hooked, the victims cannot resist doing what they are told. The criminals involved with human trafficking often beat their victims. They also subject them to emotional abuse.

Many of the victims of human trafficking—like the teen who was taken from the Haitian orphanage—are forced to live in a new country. Unable to speak the language, and without friends or family, they do not know where to go for help. They are held in secret, and have no one to turn to. These victims are also exploited economically. Some—like the Haitian girl—become servants or cooks. Others are forced to care for some-one else's children. They might do construction work or gardening and lawn care. Many females are forced into prostitution. Whatever work the victims do, they receive little—or no—money for it. The people controlling them get the rewards.

Traffickers in People

Who commits this terrible kind of crime? People of all races and ethnic groups. In fact, people often victimize members of their own racial or ethnic group, because those are people with whom they have contacts. A Salvadoran man brought young women from Central and South America to work in bars and restaurants in Texas. A group of Guatemalans illegally brought teenage girls from Guatemala into California and forced them to work as prostitutes.

Human trafficking rings often knowingly put would-be immigrants at risk of suffocating to death in vehicles with little or no air circulation. This photo shows a group of Brazilians inside a tractor-trailer after they were discovered at the border between Texas and Mexico in February 2007. The truck driver was arrested and the Brazilians were taken into custody and processed for removal back to Brazil.

HUMAN TRAFFICKING OR ILLEGAL IMMIGRATION?

Human trafficking differs from illegal immigration. In human trafficking, a criminal recruits or kidnaps victims and moves them from one place to another with the hopes of making money in some way. Illegal immigration involves persons coming from another country to the United States to live without the proper documentation registering them with the government.

Both are crimes. Sometimes they are connected. In the case of the Haitian teen, she was taken against her will and moved to another place—the United States. The criminals who moved her were guilty of human trafficking. They were also guilty of involvement in illegal immigration, however, because they brought her into the country without proper papers.

These two crimes are not always connected. Human traffickers move U.S. citizens from one state to another. In human trafficking, the person moved is the victim of a crime. Illegal immigrants may move on their own.

Members of the U.S. Coast Guard stand guard over several hundred Chinese immigrants crowded into the hold of a ship in the waters off of San Diego, California, in May 1993. The Chinese were to be illegally landed in the United States, and the Coast Guard boarded the boat when it entered U.S. waters.

Traffickers come from all walks of life. One Mexican man who held a Mexican woman as a slave also grew and sold illegal drugs. Other traffickers, however, are respected members of their communities. One of the women who enslaved the Haitian girl was a schoolteacher. Two doctors in Milwaukee forced a woman from the Philippines to work as a servant for 19 years.

Traffickers can be individuals or members of a larger group. The Mexican drug seller worked alone. The doctors in Milwaukee—both Filipinos themselves—were a married couple. Nine Guatemalans took part in the California trafficking ring. Some of these trafficking rings are active in more than one country.

The FBI Fights Human Trafficking

The FBI fights human trafficking in several ways. One is to work with state and local law enforcement officers.

In cases of trafficking, the FBI and other government agencies have an important responsibility—to help the victims. The FBI has special workers called victim specialists. They help explain to victims what rights they have. They also help victims get legal advice. They put victims in touch with groups that can help them find jobs and housing.

Many trafficking cases involve more than one country. The FBI has special offices called legal attachés (or *legats*) that work in U.S. embassies in many countries around the world. Agents in those offices smooth cooperation between U.S.-based FBI agents and foreign police. The FBI also takes part in a special joint operation to fight trafficking from parts of eastern Europe.

International cooperation proved vital in breaking one large trafficking ring that brought illegal immigrants from China to the United States. Its leader was a woman named Cheng Chui Ping. Over 10 years, she smuggled as many as

In June 1993, illegal Chinese immigrants huddle on the beach off New York City, after the freighter smuggling them ran aground. In the water, rescuers attempt to remove other immigrants from the ship. Ten of the 300 people aboard the ship drowned. Cheng Chui Ping, leader of the immigrant-smuggling operation behind the voyage, was eventually convicted on various conspiracy charges related to human smuggling, hostage taking, and fraud. She was sentenced to 35 years in prison.

Activist Shirin Shirin (front) leads a group of immigrant workers from India in a chant during a rally in front of the Department of Justice in Washington, D.C., on June 11, 2008. Shirin works to bring attention to issues affecting the well being of people from India and other nations in South Asia. The workers claimed they were victims of human trafficking.

3,000 illegal immigrants into the United States. Once they reached the country, she held them in virtual slavery until they paid back the money she charged for the transportation. She made as much as $40 million by forcing these people to pay her.

That money could not protect her from the FBI, however. Based on evidence that FBI agents gathered, Cheng was **indicted** for several crimes. She fled the country and lived on the run for several years. The FBI in the United States joined with the legat in Hong Kong and Hong Kong police to catch her. Finally, in 2003, Hong Kong police arrested Cheng. After being convicted for her crimes, she was sentenced to 35 years in prison.

Investigating Trafficking

The task of investigating human trafficking can be very difficult. Much of the evidence must come from the victims themselves. That poses many problems. They may not speak the same language as investigators. Sometimes, too, they are unwilling to speak about their treatment. They might be ashamed of being victims. Those who are in the United States illegally may fear that they will be sent back to their homeland if they speak about their treatment. When the victims are children, they might not be able to use words to describe what happened to them.

Despite all these difficulties, the FBI has succeeded in breaking many of these cases. From 2001 to 2005, the Bureau's workload in this area grew four times larger. In 2007, the Bureau arrested more than 150 people for human trafficking. That same year, its investigations led to nearly 60 convictions. With the size of the problem, though, much work remains to be done.

FAST FACTS

The U.S. State Department estimates that more than 2 million people are victims of human trafficking every year. About 18,000 of those cases are in the United States. Trafficking is a big business that may produce as much as $9 billion in profits around the world each year.

CHRONOLOGY

1910: A U.S. Department of Justice report states that the department is not interested in civil rights issues.

1923: Ku Klux Klan leader Edward Y. Clarke is indicted for transporting a woman across state lines for immoral purposes on March 1.

1956: J. Edgar Hoover tells President Eisenhower the FBI should not become involved in civil rights work.

1962: In October, the FBI launches COMIN-FIL to look for links between communists and Martin Luther King, Jr.

1963: Civil rights leader Medgar Evers is murdered on June 12; FBI agents arrest Byron De La Beckwith for the murder on June 22. Hoover approves Domestic Intelligence Division (DID) plan to gather intelligence about King's activities.

1964: Civil rights workers Michael Schwerner, Andrew Goodman, and James Chaney disappear on June 21. FBI agents arrive in Jackson, Mississippi, to open a new field office on July 5. FBI launches COINTEL-PRO aimed at learning more about the activities of the Ku Klux Klan and other white hate groups on July 30. The bodies of Schwerner, Goodman, and Chaney are discovered on August 4.

FBI carries out surveillance of Mississippi Freedom Democratic Party in late August.

FBI sends King fake tape about him in September.

1965: Nineteen men are indicted in January for conspiracy to deprive Schwerner, Goodman, and Chaney of their civil rights.

Klan members murder civil rights worker Viola Liuzzo in Alabama on March 25. Four Klan members are arrested the next day following information given by an FBI informant. Three Klan members are convicted on civil rights charges in the Liuzzo murder in December.

1967: FBI launches its "Black Nationalist Hate Groups" COINTELPRO on August 25.

In October, seven white extremists are found guilty of conspiracy to deprive Schwerner, Goodman, and Chaney of their civil rights three years earlier.

1991: FBI begins to keep statistics on hate crimes.

1994: Beckwith is finally convicted of Medgar Evers' 1963 murder.

1996: The federal government establishes the National Church Arson Task Force, which includes the FBI.

1998: FBI and other agencies in the Justice Department develop materials for teaching about hate crimes.

2005: Edgar Ray Killen is convicted on June 21 of manslaughter in the 1964 deaths of Schwerner, Goodman, and Chaney.

2007: FBI Director Robert S. Mueller announces cold case initiative to solve old civil rights cases.

GLOSSARY

activist—a person who takes vigorous action in pursuit of a political or social goal.

anti-Semitic—feeling or displaying prejudice or hostility against Jews.

appeal—a legal action in which a decision made in one court is taken to a higher court with the request that judges overturn, or reverse, the earlier decision on legal grounds.

civil rights—rights guaranteed to Americans by the U.S. Constitution, including free speech, freedom of religion, the right to vote, and the right to equal justice.

communists—people who believe in a system in which the government owns all property and makes all economic decisions; can also refer to a political party based on these beliefs.

conspiracy—a plot or an agreement to work together in a secret way to carry out crimes.

counterintelligence—a program intended to deceive enemies with false information and to learn about their plans.

defendant—a person who is required to face criminal or civil charges in court.

discrimination—unfair, unequal treatment because of a person's race, ethnic group, religion, sexual preference, or gender.

extremist—someone willing to take extreme steps to support a political position.

federal—relating to the government of the nation as a whole.

field office—an FBI office that is separate from the Bureau's main headquarters.

hate crimes—criminal acts driven by bias against a victim's race, religion, disability, ethnic origin, or sexual orientation.

indict—to formally and officially charge someone with a crime.

informant—someone who cooperates with law enforcement

officials by giving information about crimes, such as the names of those who were involved in a criminal act.

intelligence—information collected about possible threats or enemies.

jurisdiction—a legal division or area in which a court system or law enforcement agency has the authority and power to act; the FBI's jurisdiction allows it to enforce federal laws.

Ku Klux Klan—a secret organization that uses violence, intimidation, and terrorism to threaten or harm African Americans, Jews, and other racial or religious minorities.

lynching—an illegal action in which a mob hangs someone.

manslaughter—a legal term for the crime of killing someone; in the U.S. legal system, manslaughter is considered a lesser charge than murder, because the killing is done without advance planning. As a result, the penalty for a manslaughter conviction is generally less severe than a conviction for murder.

probation—placing someone who has committed a crime or other offense under supervision, usually as an alternative to jail and for a specified length of time or until he or she has shown behavior that is good enough to be taken off probation.

prosecute—to try someone in court for a crime.

prostitution—the crime of performing sex acts for money.

register—the process by which people with the right to vote become officially listed with local government offices; people must be registered in order to vote.

segregation—providing separate facilities, such as schools or sections of trains or restaurants, for people of different races.

surveillance—intense, often secret watching of people or activities.

wiretap—a connection made to a telephone wire that enables people to listen secretly to conversations held on the line.

FURTHER READING

De Capua, Sarah. *The FBI*. New York: Children's Press, 2007.

Heinrichs, Ann. *The Ku Klux Klan: A Hooded Brotherhood*. Mankato, MN: Child's World, 2002.

Holden, Henry M. *FBI 100 Years: An Unofficial History*. Minneapolis: Zenith Press, 2008.

Kessler, Ronald. *The Bureau: The Secret History of the FBI*. New York: St. Martin's Paperbacks, 2003.

McNeese, Tim. *The Civil Rights Movement: Striving for Justice*. New York: Chelsea House, 2007.

Pastan, Amy. *Martin Luther King, Jr.: A Photographic Story of a Life*. New York: DK Biographies, 2004.

Theoharis, Athan G., ed. *The FBI: A Comprehensive Reference Guide*. New York: Checkmark Books, 2000.

Winters, Robert, ed. *What Is a Hate Crime?* Farmington Hills, MI: Greenhaven Press, 2007.

INTERNET RESOURCES

http://www.civilrights.org/issues/hate
This section of the Web site of the Civil Rights Coalition for the 21st Century, an organization of 180 rights groups, has information about hate crimes and ways to build tolerance.

http://www.fbi.gov/hq/cid/civilrights/civilrts.htm
The civil rights section of the official FBI Web site has many links to detailed information on important cases and particular kinds of crimes in this area.

http://www.humantrafficking.org
This is the Web site of a nonprofit organization that aims to fight human trafficking. It includes information about that crime in the United States and around the world.

http://www.pbs.org/wgbh/amex/eyesontheprize/about/index.html
This Web site, which accompanies the PBS documentary *Eyes on the Prize*, has a wealth of information about the civil rights movement, including videos, images, profiles of major figures, descriptions of major events, and later-day comments by civil rights activists.

http://www.stanford.edu/group/King/about_king/encyclopedia
This Martin Luther King, Jr., online encyclopedia has dozens of entries on key figures and events in the civil rights movement.

http://www.usdoj.gov/
This is the official Web site of the U.S. Department of Justice.

NOTES

Chapter 1

p. 6: "We're going to see . . .": Kenneth O'Reilly, *"Racial Matters": The FBI's Secret File on Black America, 1960–1972* (New York: Free Press, 1989), p. 165.

p. 8: "Fear of the Klan . . .": O'Reilly, *"Racial Matters,"* p. 173.

p. 9: "I . . . assure you . . .": Ronald Kessler, *The Bureau: The Secret History of the FBI* (New York: St. Martin's Paperbacks, 2003), p. 152.

Chapter 2

p. 12: "find the perpetrators . . .": O'Reilly, *"Racial Matters,"* p. 197.

p. 13: "no authority . . .": O'Reilly, *"Racial Matters,"* p. 9.

p. 16: "Men have been taken . . .": Henry M. Holden, *FBI 100 Years: An Unofficial History* (Minneapolis: Zenith Press, 2008), p. 106.

p. 20: "Edgar, I want . . .": O'Reilly, *"Racial Matters,"* p. 199.

p. 22: "Protecting the civil rights . . .": FBI online news story, "Civil Rights: FBI Announces Partnership in Reviewing Cold Cases," February 27, 2007. http://www.fbi.gov/page2/feb07/coldcase022707.htm.

Chapter 3

p. 23: "No matter what kind . . .": O'Reilly, *"Racial Matters,"* p. 63.

p. 29: "The Director . . .": O'Reilly, *"Racial Matters,"* p. 130.

p. 29: "most dangerous Negro . . .": Kessler, *The Bureau*, p. 157.

p. 31: "most notorious liar . . .": Athan G. Theoharis, ed., *The FBI: A Comprehensive Reference Guide* (New York: Checkmark Books, 2000), p. 123.

p. 32: "the greatest threat . . .": Holden, *FBI 100 Years*, p. 120.

Chapter 4

p. 34: "Remember 9/11 . . .": FBI online news story, "Decidedly Uncivil, Part 2: Muslim Mother Target of Hate Crime," May 2, 2007. http://www.fbi.gov/page2/may07/hate050207.htm.

p. 35: "against a person . . .": FBI, "Hate Crime—Overview" (undated). http://www.fbi.gov/hq/cid/civilrights/overview.htm.

p. 38: "It sends a very powerful . . .": FBI online news story, "Lesson in Tolerance: Civil Rights Group Sponsors Traveling Exhibit," April 14, 2008. http://www.fbi.gov/page2/april08/traveling_trunk041408.html.

Chapter 5

p. 47: "subject[ed] the victim . . .": Richard G. Schott, "Double Exposure: Civil Liability and Criminal Prosecution in Federal Court for Police Misconduct," *FBI Law Enforcement Bulletin* (May 2008), p. 30.

Chapter 6

p. 49: "I applaud the courage . . .": FBI, Miami Field Division press release, "Schoolteacher and Ex-Husband Sentenced for Human Trafficking and Smuggling Charges," May 20, 2008. http://miami.fbi.gov/dojpressrel/pressrel08/mm200805020.htm.

p. 50: "These young women . . .": FBI, Los Angeles Field Division press release, "Nine Charged in Sex Trafficking Ring Involving Minors," August 9, 2007. http://losangeles.fbi.gov/dojpressrel/pressrel07/la080907usa.htm.

INDEX

Numbers in **bold italics** refer to captions.

About the Author

Dale Anderson lives in eastern Pennsylvania, where he has written dozens of books on history and other subjects. He enjoys cooking, bird watching, movies, puzzles, and sports. He has written three other books in this series.